ALL ABOUT ME.

MILLENNIUM EDITION

BY PHILIPP KEEL

BROADWAY BOOKS

NEW YORK

BROADWAY

Broadway Books titles may be purchased for business or promotional use or for special sales. For information, please write to: Special Markets Department, Random House, Inc., 1540 Broadway, New York, NY 10036.

BROADWAY BOOKS and its logo, a letter B bisected on the diagonal, are trademarks of Broadway Books, a division of Random House, Inc.

Visit our website at www.broadwaybooks.com

Library of Congress Cataloging-in-Publication Data
Keel, Philipp.
    All about me, Millennium Edition.   /   by Philipp Keel. — 1st ed.
        p.   cm.
    ISBN 0-7679-0412-5
    1. Self-disclosure.   I. Title
    [BF697.5.S427K44   1997]
    155.2'83— dc21   97-27948
                        CIP

FIRST EDITION

Edited by Tamar Halpern

99 00 01 02 03 10 9 8 7 6 5 4 3 2 1

CONTENTS

With questions you not only reveal your curiosity to others, you also invite others to express their feelings, wishes, and fears; you show a genuine interest in and respect for their lives. This book is a neutral tool that allows you to comfortably ask and answer questions with friends, partners, family, colleagues, chance acquaintances – or simply with yourself.

However you choose to use the book – as a journal, a communication tool, a game – try to answer spontaneously. The first answer that comes to mind is probably the best. Fortunately we constantly develop and change. Some of our thoughts, beliefs, and ideas may shift within a few months or years. As you travel through the book, you will make discoveries about others and about yourself. And even if you find that you never want to ask or answer another question again, you will at least have discovered this much from your *All About Me.*

This book is dedicated to everyone who has not asked enough questions of others, and to those who have never been asked.

– Philipp Keel

Name: _____

Address: _____

Phone number: _____

Today's date: _____

Place of birth: _____

Date of birth: _____

Astrological sign: _____

Profession: _____

Education: _____

Height: _____ Weight: _____

Hair color: _____ Eye color: _____

Distinguishing marks: _____

Blood type: _____ Allergies: _____

_____

Mother's full name: _____

Date of birth: _____

Father's full name: _____

Date of birth: _____

Mother's maiden name: _____

Siblings' names: Ages:

_____   _____

_____   _____

_____   _____

Names of maternal grandparents: _____

Names of paternal grandparents: _____

Mother's family comes from: _____

Father's family comes from: _____

Famous or notable relative or ancestor: _____

MILLENNIUM

Where and with whom will you be when the clock strikes midnight on Millennium's Eve?

Where: _____   With whom: _____

Where and with whom would you most like to be when the clock strikes midnight?

Where: _____   With whom: _____

Do you feel privileged to enter the new Millennium? _____

One Millennium resolution you will probably break: _____

_____

One Millennium resolution you swear to keep: _____

_____

One wish for the world in the new Millennium: _____

_____

One fear you have about the world in the new Millennium: _____

_____

One thing you would have liked to have accomplished before the new Millennium:

_____

A social behavior that should be banned in the new Millennium: _____

_____

A phrase or saying that should be banned in the new Millennium: _____

_____

A product or brand that should be banned in the new Millennium: _____

_____

An invention that would make your life easier in the new Millennium: _____

_____

Predictions for the new Millennium:

A Hilton on the moon.

    [ ] Within 25 years.   [ ] Within 100 years.   [ ] In the next century.   [ ] Never.

Cure for cancer and AIDS over the counter.

    [ ] Within 25 years.   [ ] Within 100 years.   [ ] In the next century.   [ ] Never.

Empty highways.

    [ ] Within 25 years.   [ ] Within 100 years.   [ ] In the next century.   [ ] Never.

No more canned or frozen food.

    [ ] Within 25 years.   [ ] Within 100 years.   [ ] In the next century.   [ ] Never.

Third World War.

[ ] Within 25 years.　[ ] Within 100 years.　[ ] In the next century.　[ ] Never.

Most people reach the age of 125.

[ ] Within 25 years.　[ ] Within 100 years.　[ ] In the next century.　[ ] Never.

Politicians truly serve the public.

[ ] Within 25 years.　[ ] Within 100 years.　[ ] In the next century.　[ ] Never.

Imported bottled water is illegal.

[ ] Within 25 years.　[ ] Within 100 years.　[ ] In the next century.　[ ] Never.

Good men are easier to find.

[ ] Within 25 years.　[ ] Within 100 years.　[ ] In the next century.　[ ] Never.

Lightbulbs are only for sale in antique stores.

[ ] Within 25 years.　[ ] Within 100 years.　[ ] In the next century.　[ ] Never.

A maximum of two children per family.

[ ] Within 25 years.　[ ] Within 100 years.　[ ] In the next century.　[ ] Never.

Extinction of magazines and books.

[ ] Within 25 years.　[ ] Within 100 years.　[ ] In the next century.　[ ] Never.

World peace and prejudice are no longer issues.

[ ] Within 25 years.　[ ] Within 100 years.　[ ] In the next century.　[ ] Never.

Post offices are not a hassle.

[ ] Within 25 years.　[ ] Within 100 years.　[ ] In the next century.　[ ] Never.

All drugs are legalized.

    [ ] Within 25 years.   [ ] Within 100 years.   [ ] In the next century.   [ ] Never.

Africa is the richest country in the world.

    [ ] Within 25 years.   [ ] Within 100 years.   [ ] In the next century.   [ ] Never.

Lawyers are genuinely nice people.

    [ ] Within 25 years.   [ ] Within 100 years.   [ ] In the next century.   [ ] Never.

Americans speak more than one language.

    [ ] Within 25 years.   [ ] Within 100 years.   [ ] In the next century.   [ ] Never.

Bill Gates buys his own country.

    [ ] Within 25 years.   [ ] Within 100 years.   [ ] In the next century.   [ ] Never.

Old-fashioned lifestyle becomes fashionable.

    [ ] Within 25 years.   [ ] Within 100 years.   [ ] In the next century.   [ ] Never.

The Catholic Church approves of birth control.

    [ ] Within 25 years.   [ ] Within 100 years.   [ ] In the next century.   [ ] Never.

America is less corporate.

    [ ] Within 25 years.   [ ] Within 100 years.   [ ] In the next century.   [ ] Never.

Admission tickets are needed to visit the centers of world capitols.

    [ ] Within 25 years.   [ ] Within 100 years.   [ ] In the next century.   [ ] Never.

Everything is sponsored by advertising.

    [ ] Within 25 years.   [ ] Within 100 years.   [ ] In the next century.   [ ] Never.

Homosexuality is integrated in every society in the world.

[ ] Within 25 years.   [ ] Within 100 years.   [ ] In the next century.   [ ] Never.

Flowers, fruits, and vegetables grow in one day.

[ ] Within 25 years.   [ ] Within 100 years.   [ ] In the next century.   [ ] Never.

Pet-sized elephants.

[ ] Within 25 years.   [ ] Within 100 years.   [ ] In the next century.   [ ] Never.

Contact with beings from outer space.

[ ] Within 25 years.   [ ] Within 100 years.   [ ] In the next century.   [ ] Never.

Disney purchases Egypt and turns it into a theme park.

[ ] Within 25 years.   [ ] Within 100 years.   [ ] In the next century.   [ ] Never.

Vegas goes bankrupt.

[ ] Within 25 years.   [ ] Within 100 years.   [ ] In the next century.   [ ] Never.

Human waste is recycled into energy.

[ ] Within 25 years.   [ ] Within 100 years.   [ ] In the next century.   [ ] Never.

All races have completely mixed.

[ ] Within 25 years.   [ ] Within 100 years.   [ ] In the next century.   [ ] Never.

Plastic surgery is as common as getting a haircut.

[ ] Within 25 years.   [ ] Within 100 years.   [ ] In the next century.   [ ] Never.

Life is beautiful.

[ ] Within 25 years.   [ ] Within 100 years.   [ ] In the next century.   [ ] Never.

If your voice could broadcast all over the world at midnight 2000, what would you say?

_____

What kinds of choices will you make in the new Millennium?

[ ] e-mail	or	[ ] letter.
[ ] Theme park	or	[ ] forest.
[ ] Poker	or	[ ] Tarot cards.
[ ] Fashion	or	[ ] soul.
[ ] Catalog	or	[ ] store.
[ ] Gym	or	[ ] hiking.
[ ] Library	or	[ ] Internet.
[ ] Cigarettes	or	[ ] oral sex.
[ ] Discovery Channel	or	[ ] safari.
[ ] Venus	or	[ ] Mars.
[ ] Religion	or	[ ] meditation.
[ ] Success	or	[ ] time.
[ ] Pets	or	[ ] kids.
[ ] Frisbee	or	[ ] UFO.
[ ] Drugs	or	[ ] personal confrontation.
[ ] Either	or	[ ] neither.

Is 2000 more than just another year?   [ ] Yes   [ ] No

If no, why?   _____

Does the end of the Millennium signify the beginning of something new?   [ ] Yes   [ ] No

If yes, what?   _____

What do you consider to be your greatest achievement before the new Millennium?

_____

Who is the first person you will most likely have sex with in the new Millennium?

_____

What will most likely be your final year in the new Millennium? _____

How do you think the Y2K Bug will affect your life? _____

_____

What comes to mind when you read the word MILLENNIUM? _____

_____

If you don't have children yet, do you regret not having

any before the new Millennium?   [ ] Yes   [ ] No

If yes, why? _____

Do you believe that the pace of life will slow down?   [ ] Yes   [ ] No

Do you believe human beings are becoming more aware

of themselves and others?   [ ] Yes   [ ] No

You will say farewell to the last Millennium:

[ ] with a kiss.   [ ] with a tear.

[ ] with a kick.   [ ] with a shrug.

You will welcome the new millennium:

[ ] with a kiss.   [ ] with a tear.

[ ] with a kick.   [ ] with a shrug.

What will change in the new Millennium?

Car dealers:	[ ] better	[ ] worse
World hunger:	[ ] better	[ ] worse
Holiday destinations:	[ ] better	[ ] worse
Manners:	[ ] better	[ ] worse
Pollution:	[ ] better	[ ] worse
Art/Design:	[ ] better	[ ] worse
Health:	[ ] better	[ ] worse
Christmas:	[ ] better	[ ] worse
Unemployment rate:	[ ] better	[ ] worse
Parents:	[ ] better	[ ] worse
Customer service:	[ ] better	[ ] worse
Product quality:	[ ] better	[ ] worse
Big Mac:	[ ] better	[ ] worse
Movies:	[ ] better	[ ] worse
Soul-mate search:	[ ] better	[ ] worse
Education:	[ ] better	[ ] worse
Public bathrooms:	[ ] better	[ ] worse

Toys: [ ] better   [ ] worse

News: [ ] better   [ ] worse

Celine Dion: [ ] better   [ ] worse

What will you most likely miss about the last century? _____

_____

Something you would like to experience on January 1, 2000: _____

_____

A recent fantasy you've had about the future: _____

_____

Will the human race reach the end of the new Millennium?   [ ] Yes   [ ] No

Who will become the next Mozart? _____

What will replace oil? _____

What will replace dictators? _____

What will replace computers? _____

What will replace the desire to explore the world? _____

_____

What will replace cigarettes? _____

What will be more important than environmental issues? _____

_____

What will replace armies? _____

What will replace the fear of cancer and AIDS? _____

What will replace the curiosity of exploring the Internet? _____

What will replace the challenge to conquer the peak of Mount Everest? _____

_____

What will replace the wish to win the lottery? _____

What will replace the trend of self-improvement? _____

What will replace tradition? _____

F A V O R I T E S

Although you may not have an "absolute favorite,"
answer the following questions spontaneously. The best answer
will be the first thought that comes to mind.

A color you like to wear: _____

Regardless of size or circumstance, an animal you would like to own as a pet:

_____

A flower you would like to grow in your garden: _____

Your lucky number: _____

A smell that makes you pause: _____

A taste that makes you melt: _____

A hobby that occupies your time: _____

A sport you enjoy watching: _____

A sport you enjoy playing: _____

A city you like to visit: _____

A country you like to explore: _____

F A V O R I T E S

Your favorite meal: _____

A drink you often order: _____

A delicious dessert: _____

A game you like to play: _____

A book you strongly recommend: _____

An author who has affected you: _____

The magazine you read most frequently: _____

The newspaper you prefer to read on Sundays: _____

Music you prefer to listen to when you are alone: _____

The singer or band you currently listen to the most:

_____

The film you could watch over and over: _____

_____

A director you admire: _____

F A V O R I T E S

An actress whose performances you admire: _____

An actor whose performances you admire: _____

A TV show you watch regularly: _____

An artist whose work you highly respect: _____

A piece of clothing you love to wear: _____

A monument you would like to have a view of from your bedroom:

_____

Your favorite time of day: _____

Your favorite place to sit at home: _____

What you most like to do on Sunday: _____

_____

Your motto: _____

_____

_____

Your children: Ages:

_____   _____

_____   _____

_____   _____

Your pets: _____

You live in a _____

Your transportation: _____

Your approximate annual income: _____

    [ ] You are making more money than ever before.

    [ ] You always thought you would make more money.

    [ ] You never expected to make this much money.

Approximate number of hours you spend working each week: _____

    [ ] You wish it were less.   [ ] You wish it were more.

THE FRUITS OF YOUR LABOR

Your watch: _____

Your cologne or perfume: _____

Something important on your desk: _____

On your wall hangs _____

Under your bed or in your closet you hide _____

Something important on your night table: _____

When you sleep, you wear _____

If you had a safe, you would keep _____

Things you like to buy: _____

_____

If you could afford it at this moment, you would buy _____

_____

You collect _____

You don't have a lot of _____

Your strangest possession: _____

Your most expensive possession: _____

Your prized possession: _____

Material possessions are _____

If your house was burning and you only had time to rescue three things,

they would be:

1 _____

2 _____

3 _____

M O R A L S

Something forbidden you have done that might even surprise your closest friends:

_____

People should not marry before this age: _____

People should not have children before this age: _____

The appropriate age for having sex: _____

The first time you had sex, you were this age: _____

Your most recent lie: _____

When you are late for an appointment and it's your fault, you

     [ ] tell a white lie.   [ ] tell the truth.

A lie you tell yourself: _____

_____

Something you have stolen that was not worth the risk: _____

_____

MORALS

One person you have killed in your thoughts:

_____

One person you might kill if you knew the law would protect you:

_____

One thing in this world you are addicted to: _____

A drug or alcoholic beverage you take on a regular basis:

_____

If there were no side effects, you would enjoy being addicted to:

_____

Drugs you have tried in the past: _____

A drug you would never try: _____

A drug you will never try again: _____

You believe hitting a child is an appropriate form of discipline.   [ ] Yes   [ ] No

MORALS

As an adult, you have hit a woman.   [ ] Yes   [ ] No

If yes, why? _____

As an adult, you have hit a man.   [ ] Yes   [ ] No

If yes, why? _____

You have been arrested.   [ ] Yes   [ ] No

If yes, for what? _____

You have read someone's diary or gone through someone's
private belongings without permission.   [ ] Yes   [ ] No

If yes, which best describes your reason?

    [ ] jealousy   [ ] distrust   [ ] curiosity

    [ ] you were asked by someone else to do it

If yes, what did you discover? _____

MORALS

What would your reaction be if your spouse or partner cheated on you? _____

_____

You have cheated.   [ ] Yes   [ ] No

A time you purposely hurt someone emotionally: _____

_____

You have apologized.   [ ] Yes   [ ] No

A time you accidentally hurt someone emotionally: _____

_____

You have apologized.   [ ] Yes   [ ] No

You owe someone money but have stalled in paying it back.   [ ] Yes   [ ] No

If yes, what is the amount? _____

G O D A N D T H E W O R L D

Do you believe in God?   [ ] Yes   [ ] No

Describe God: _____

_____

What religion were you raised with? _____

Do you practice this religion?   [ ] Yes   [ ] No

Your most spiritual moment: _____

That last time you were in a house of worship: _____

Death is: _____

_____

How you picture the end of the world: _____

_____

God has spoken to you.   [ ] Yes   [ ] No

If yes, what did God tell you? _____

_____

Do you feel that most wars started because of religious conflicts?　　[ ] Yes　[ ] No

Does life exist on other planets?　　[ ] Yes　[ ] No

Have they made contact with us?　　[ ] Yes　[ ] No

Do you believe we are descendants of Adam and Eve?　　[ ] Yes　[ ] No

Do you believe in evolution?　　[ ] Yes　[ ] No

Do you believe in astrology?　　[ ] Yes　[ ] No

Do you read your horoscope?　　[ ] Yes　[ ] No

If yes, why? _____

Have you ever been treated by a psychotherapist?　　[ ] Yes　[ ] No

If yes, why? _____

Do you believe in reincarnation?　　[ ] Yes　[ ] No

If reincarnation does exist, you would like to come back as:

_____

What is your opinion of

    the right to have an abortion: [ ] Pro   [ ] Con

    the right to own guns: [ ] Pro   [ ] Con

    the welfare system: [ ] Pro   [ ] Con

    the death penalty: [ ] Pro   [ ] Con

    rights and services for illegal immigrants: [ ] Pro   [ ] Con

    legalization of drugs: [ ] Pro   [ ] Con

    equal rights for homosexuals: [ ] Pro   [ ] Con

    the practice of premarital sex: [ ] Pro   [ ] Con

Which issue concerns you the most?

(You can choose from the above list or write your own answer.)

On behalf of this issue, you have

    [ ] donated time.   [ ] donated money.   [ ] done nothing.

The first step toward resolving poverty: _____

_____

The first step toward resolving racism: _____

_____

The environmental issue that concerns you the most: _____

_____

Do you believe a person is defined

by what she or he does for a living?   [ ] Yes   [ ] No

Why? _____

Politically, you define yourself as

    [ ] liberal.   [ ] moderate.   [ ] conservative.

The worst crime against humanity: _____

The worst political crime: _____

The minimum punishment for those who molest children should be: _____

_____

The minimum punishment for those who rape should be: _____

_____

Your opinion of the military: _____

_____

Your opinion of the draft: _____

_____

You would fight in a war if _____

_____

Three things you like about your mother:

1 _____

2 _____

3 _____

Three things you like about your father:

1 _____

2 _____

3 _____

Which question felt easier to answer?   [ ] Mother   [ ] Father

Character or physical traits you inherited from your mother: _____

_____

_____

Three things you dislike about your mother:

1 _____

2 _____

3 _____

Three things you dislike about your father:

1 _____

2 _____

3 _____

Which question felt easier to answer?   [ ] Mother   [ ] Father

Character or physical traits you inherited from your father: _____

_____

_____

When you were a child, your parents spent

[ ] enough time with you.

[ ] too much time with you.

[ ] not enough time with you.

The most common issue you and your parents have argued about: _____

_____

Your most beautiful childhood memory of your parents: _____

_____

Your most horrifying childhood memory of your parents: _____

_____

If you didn't know your parents, you would choose these two people

as your mother and your father:

Mother: _____

Father: _____

If they were not available, you would choose these two famous people
as your mother and your father:

Mother: _____

Father: _____

Do you think you said "I love you" enough to your mother?   [ ] Yes   [ ] No

Do you think you said "I love you" enough to your father?   [ ] Yes   [ ] No

Has your mother told you that she loves you enough?   [ ] Yes   [ ] No

Has your father told you that he loves you enough?   [ ] Yes   [ ] No

Your mother often said: _____

_____

Your father often said: _____

_____

Whom do you resemble physically?   [ ] Mother   [ ] Father

Something your parents did that you have never forgiven: _____

_____

What would it take for you to forgive them? _____

_____

If you had to imagine your mother as an animal, she would be:

_____

If you had to imagine your father as an animal, he would be:

_____

You and your siblings share in common: _____

A trait you do not share with your siblings: _____

Your favorite relative is: _____

Why? _____

Your least favorite relative is: _____

Why? _____

F A M I L Y

If you were not related to your family members, you would still choose these three as your friends:

1 _____

2 _____

3 _____

If you had to imagine your siblings as animals, they would be:

Name   Animal

_____   _____

_____   _____

_____   _____

_____   _____

Something you wish for your mother: _____

_____

Something you wish for your father: _____

_____

Three traits you look for in a friend:

1 _____

2 _____

3 _____

The friend you have known for the longest amount of time:

_____   Number of years: _____

Is this person a close friend?   [ ] Yes   [ ] No

Why or why not? _____

The friend you miss the most: _____

When was the last time you saw this friend? _____

When do you think you will see this friend again? _____

A friend who makes you laugh often: _____

A friend to whom you can tell anything: _____

F R I E N D S

A friend to whom you can go for advice: _____

The best piece of advice this friend gave you: _____

A friend you can have adventures with: _____

The best adventure you had with this friend: _____

_____

A friend you can flirt with: _____

A friend you should not flirt with as much as you do: _____

_____

A friend you would like to kiss: _____

A friend you should not have kissed: _____

A friend you don't take seriously: _____

A friend you may lose soon: _____

Why? _____

F R I E N D S

A friend you lost for a reason other than death: _____

    [   ] You hope to see this friend again.

    [   ] You hope never to see this friend again.

    [   ] If you were to see this friend again, you would be unaffected.

A friend who does or believes in something you cannot respect:

_____

Describe what it is that you cannot respect: _____

_____

A friend with whom you would like to be closer: _____

Describe the barrier that exists between you and this friend: _____

_____

A friend to whom you would never lend money: _____

Why? _____

A friend who has betrayed you: _____

How did this friend betray you? _____

Have you forgiven this friend?   [ ] Yes   [ ] No

A friend who has done something terrible but whom you have forgiven:

_____

Describe what you have forgiven: _____

_____

A friend you need to forgive: _____

A friend you would name as godparent of your child: _____

A friend to whom you have something important to say, but have not yet had the courage:

_____

What is it that you want to say? _____

_____

F R I E N D S

Your two closest friends:

1 _____

2 _____

One trait you admire in each of them:

1 _____

2 _____

One trait you wish each of them could change:

1 _____

2 _____

An animal that best describes each of them:

1 _____

2 _____

Your mother is your friend.   [ ] Yes   [ ] No

Your father is your friend.   [ ] Yes   [ ] No

Your best friend as a child: _____

Your worst enemy as a child: _____

Your best friend as a teenager: _____

Your worst enemy as a teenager: _____

(If you are not yet an adult, leave this blank until you are an adult - then fill out a new All About Me.*)*

Your best friend as an adult: _____

Your worst enemy as an adult: _____

If you could, where would you banish your worst enemy to?

_____

Are you able to forgive your enemies?   [ ] Yes   [ ] No

If no, why not? _____

F R I E N D S

The friend who is most like you: _____

Why? _____

The friend who is most unlike you: _____

Why? _____

The friend who uses most of your energy: _____

A friend you will see in hell: _____

A friend you will see in heaven: _____

E G O

Your three best qualities:

1 _____

2 _____

3 _____

Your three worst qualities:

1 _____

2 _____

3 _____

Of these three worst qualities, which one do you struggle with most frequently?

[ ] 1   [ ] 2   [ ] 3

Which of the three worst qualities have you tried to change?

[ ] 1   [ ] 2   [ ] 3

E G O

Three words that describe how others view you:

1 _____

2 _____

3 _____

Three words you would use to describe your ideal self:

1 _____

2 _____

3 _____

Three things for which you are often complimented:

1 _____

2 _____

3 _____

Which one of the three is most meaningful to you?

[ ] *1*   [ ] *2*   [ ] *3*

E G O

A special compliment that made you blush: _____

_____

Who gave you this special compliment? _____

An insult that made you burn: _____

_____

What was your reaction to this insult? _____

You are far better than most people you know at: _____

_____

The animal that best describes you: _____

You are embarrassed when others: _____

You are embarrassed when you: _____

Others are embarrassed when you: _____

The greatest amount of physical pain you have ever endured: _____

_____

EGO

The greatest amount of emotional pain you have ever endured: _____

_____

Your proudest moment: _____

_____

Someone who shared this moment with you: _____

The moment you are most ashamed of: _____

Someone who shared this moment with you: _____

When discussing your career with others, you tend to

    [ ] exaggerate.   [ ] understate.   [ ] be factual.

When discussing your love life with others, you tend to

    [ ] exaggerate.   [ ] understate.   [ ] be factual.

When telling stories or relaying the details of your day, you tend to

    [ ] exaggerate.   [ ] understate.   [ ] be factual.

E G O

If you didn't have commitments to others, you would _____

_____

The number of drinks that constitutes your limit: _____

Your best physical feature: _____

You have considered plastic surgery.   [ ] Yes   [ ] No

At your best, you are most like this famous person: _____

_____

At your worst, you are most like this famous person: _____

_____

Create a newspaper headline you would like to read about yourself: _____

_____

Your most recent selfless act: _____

_____

W H A T   Y O U   L I K E

Spontaneously list anything that comes to mind.

W H A T Y O U D I S L I K E

Spontaneously list anything that comes to mind.

You keep a diary.	[ ] Yes	[ ] No
You like to cook.	[ ] Yes	[ ] No
You exercise regularly.	[ ] Yes	[ ] No
You sketch while you are on the phone.	[ ] Yes	[ ] No
You have read a book in the past month.	[ ] Yes	[ ] No
You replace the toilet-paper roll immediately.	[ ] Yes	[ ] No
You like crossword puzzles.	[ ] Yes	[ ] No
You have visited the Eiffel Tower.	[ ] Yes	[ ] No
You have a secret you have never shared with anyone.	[ ] Yes	[ ] No
You wait until the last minute to fill your car with gas.	[ ] Yes	[ ] No
You snore.	[ ] Yes	[ ] No
You have been to your ancestors' homeland.	[ ] Yes	[ ] No
You read in the bathroom.	[ ] Yes	[ ] No
Being sick is a vacation.	[ ] Yes	[ ] No
You often have people over at your house.	[ ] Yes	[ ] No
You like America.	[ ] Yes	[ ] No
You can remember jokes.	[ ] Yes	[ ] No
You play cards.	[ ] Yes	[ ] No
You fold your underwear.	[ ] Yes	[ ] No
You talk in your sleep.	[ ] Yes	[ ] No
You eat fast.	[ ] Yes	[ ] No
You recycle small batteries.	[ ] Yes	[ ] No

You often avoid paying full price.   [ ] Yes   [ ] No

You like hiking.   [ ] Yes   [ ] No

You like being on the phone.   [ ] Yes   [ ] No

You shave regularly.   [ ] Yes   [ ] No

You set your watch a few minutes ahead.   [ ] Yes   [ ] No

You are always late.   [ ] Yes   [ ] No

You often get headaches.   [ ] Yes   [ ] No

You smoke.   [ ] Yes   [ ] No

A naked photo of you exists.   [ ] Yes   [ ] No

You can whistle.   [ ] Yes   [ ] No

You write letters regularly.   [ ] Yes   [ ] No

You believe in destiny.   [ ] Yes   [ ] No

You brush your teeth three times a day.   [ ] Yes   [ ] No

You have something you wish to confess.   [ ] Yes   [ ] No

You change your bedsheets weekly.   [ ] Yes   [ ] No

You bite your fingernails.   [ ] Yes   [ ] No

You pick your nose.   [ ] Yes   [ ] No

You are a vegetarian.   [ ] Yes   [ ] No

You have eaten in a restaurant alone.   [ ] Yes   [ ] No

You have gone to a movie alone.   [ ] Yes   [ ] No

You have taken a vacation alone.   [ ] Yes   [ ] No

You read the newspaper every day.   [ ] Yes   [ ] No

You have not used a hair dryer in the past five years.   [ ] Yes   [ ] No

You have never used a personal computer.   [ ] Yes   [ ] No

You have made love in an airplane.   [ ] Yes   [ ] No

You have hit your father or mother in anger.   [ ] Yes   [ ] No

When you think you have done something

    wrong, you are quick to apologize.   [ ] Yes   [ ] No

You lose control in heated arguments.   [ ] Yes   [ ] No

In the morning when your alarm clock sounds,

    you get out of bed immediately.   [ ] Yes   [ ] No

You drank mother's milk.   [ ] Yes   [ ] No

You generally save letters and postcards.   [ ] Yes   [ ] No

You hate parties.   [ ] Yes   [ ] No

You have stolen money from your parents.   [ ] Yes   [ ] No

You have fired a gun.   [ ] Yes   [ ] No

You often have the last word.   [ ] Yes   [ ] No

Less is more.   [ ] Yes   [ ] No

You give money to homeless people.   [ ] Yes   [ ] No

Money has influenced your character.   [ ] Yes   [ ] No

You know who you are.   [ ] Yes   [ ] No

You enjoy being photographed.   [ ] Yes   [ ] No

Life treats you well.   [ ] Yes   [ ] No

Three people you consider to be geniuses:

1 _____

2 _____

3 _____

Three inventions you consider to be ingenius:

1 _____

2 _____

3 _____

Your three favorite childhood toys or games:

1 _____

2 _____

3 _____

T O P   T H R E E

Three words you use often when speaking:

1 _____

2 _____

3 _____

Three sounds that disturb you:

1 _____

2 _____

3 _____

Three lessons you have learned the hard way:

1 _____

2 _____

3 _____

Three things you would never do:

1 _____

2 _____

3 _____

Three charities or people to whom you would donate money:

1 _____

2 _____

3 _____

Three things you would not allow your children to do:

1 _____

2 _____

3 _____

T O P T H R E E

Three things you have done in your life that you regret:

1 _____

2 _____

3 _____

Three things for which you are thankful:

1 _____

2 _____

3 _____

Your dream: _____

Your hope: _____

If you had the talent or the opportunity, you would _____

_____

Something you wish you could learn with the snap of your fingers: _____

_____

Something you wish you could change about your life: _____

_____

Something you wish you could change about yourself: _____

_____

You wish you had been born into a different race.   [ ] Yes   [ ] No

You wish you had been born into a different religion.   [ ] Yes   [ ] No

You wish you had been born as the opposite sex.   [ ] Yes   [ ] No

W I S H E S   A N D   D R E A M S

Someone's diary you would love to read: _____

Three qualities your ideal man or woman should possess:

1 _____

2 _____

3 _____

Three qualities your ideal relationship should have:

1 _____

2 _____

3 _____

You want to retire at this age: _____

How you plan to spend the last years of your life: _____

_____

How you would like to spend the last minutes of your life: _____

_____

W I S H E S A N D D R E A M S

For your last dinner, you would like to invite these five people:

1 _____

2 _____

3 _____

4 _____

5 _____

The menu for your last dinner might be:

Appetizer: _____

Main course: _____

Dessert: _____

At your funeral, you want people to remember you as _____

_____

W I S H E S   A N D   D R E A M S

Someone who should not, under any circumstances, speak at your funeral:

_____

Someone you would like to have speak at your funeral:

_____

A dream you have had more than once: _____

_____

_____

Something you dreamed that later happened or turned out to be true: _____

_____

_____

E M O T I O N S

The emotion you tend to hide the most: _____

The emotion you seem to experience the most: _____

The predominant emotion you have experienced lately: _____

A moment when you achieved absolute happiness: _____

_____

You have a great amount of guilt regarding _____

_____

You would feel envious right now if _____

_____

A piece of music that makes you sentimental: _____

_____

The music reminds you of: _____

_____

EMOTIONS

When you are happy, you need _____

When you are sad, you need _____

When you are sentimental, you need _____

When you are angry, you need _____

When you are in love, you need _____

When you are lonely, you need _____

You would jump up and down and shout with joy right now if someone told you:

_____

The last time you were very angry was when _____

_____

The last time you cried uncontrollably was when _____

_____

A moment in your life when your emotions froze and you felt absolutely nothing:

_____

EMOTIONS

Someone who genuinely makes or has made you happy: _____

_____

Something that makes you happy: _____

You get angry with yourself when you _____

_____

Someone or something that made you laugh this week: _____

_____

Write the colors that match the following emotions for you:

Fear _____   Love _____

Happiness _____   Sadness _____

Anger _____   Guilt _____

Jealousy _____   Loneliness _____

MEMORIES

Your earliest memory: _____

When you were a child, you believed: _____

_____

Do you still believe this?   [ ] Yes   [ ] No

Your first kiss.

When: _____   Where: _____

With whom: _____

The first time you fell in love.

When: _____   Where: _____

With whom: _____

The last time you fell in love.

When: _____   Where: _____

With whom: _____

M E M O R I E S

Describe your first paying job: _____

_____ How old were you? _____

Describe your best paying job: _____

_____ How old were you? _____

Your most vivid childhood memory: _____

_____

You are haunted by the memory of: _____

_____

The memory that still makes you laugh: _____

_____

A person who was exceptionally kind to you: _____

_____

A person who made you miserable for a long time: _____

_____

MEMORIES

One of your most peaceful moments: _____

_____

Your best birthday: _____

One of your most tragic memories: _____

_____

One of your most jealous moments: _____

_____

One of your angriest memories: _____

_____

Your worst birthday: _____

One of your most desperate moments: _____

_____

Someone you wish you had never met: _____

M E M O R I E S

One of your most driven moments: _____

_____

The memory or story you tend to exaggerate when telling to others: _____

_____

One of your most embarrassing moments: _____

_____

A smell that reminds you of your childhood: _____

_____

An object you still own or remember vividly from your childhood: _____

_____

A routine you remember from your childhood: _____

_____

CHOICES

[ ] Sunrise   or   [ ] sunset.   [ ] Open   or   [ ] closed.

[ ] Sweet   or   [ ] sour.   [ ] Bath   or   [ ] shower.

[ ] Sahara   or   [ ] Himalaya.   [ ] Square   or   [ ] circle.

[ ] Dolphin   or   [ ] eagle.   [ ] Fire   or   [ ] water.

[ ] Old   or   [ ] new.   [ ] Lightning   or   [ ] thunder.

[ ] Hot   or   [ ] cold.   [ ] Black   or   [ ] white.

[ ] Coke   or   [ ] Pepsi.   [ ] Ocean   or   [ ] forest.

[ ] Soft   or   [ ] hard.   [ ] Dogs   or   [ ] cats.

[ ] Train   or   [ ] plane.   [ ] Day   or   [ ] night.

[ ] Yesterday or   [ ] tomorrow.   [ ] Leaves   or   [ ] roots.

[ ] Red   or   [ ] blue.   [ ] Left   or   [ ] right.

[ ] Fast   or   [ ] slow.   [ ] Cremation   or   [ ] burial.

[ ] Beatles   or   [ ] Elvis.   [ ] Victim   or   [ ] criminal.

[ ] Blind   or   [ ] deaf.   [ ] Even   or   [ ] odd.

[ ] Written or [ ] spoken.   [ ] Sun or [ ] rain.

[ ] Woman or [ ] man.   [ ] Briefs or [ ] boxers.

[ ] Carpet or [ ] hardwood floor.   [ ] Pen or [ ] pencil.

[ ] Earthquake or [ ] hurricane.   [ ] Horns or [ ] strings.

[ ] City or [ ] countryside.   [ ] Summer or [ ] winter.

[ ] Vanilla or [ ] chocolate.   [ ] Horizontal or [ ] vertical.

[ ] Abstract or [ ] figurative.   [ ] Destiny or [ ] choice.

[ ] Limited or [ ] open-ended.   [ ] Alone or [ ] together.

[ ] House or [ ] condominium.   [ ] New York or [ ] Paris.

[ ] ! or [ ] ?   [ ] Silver or [ ] gold.

F E A R S

Things you fear:

    [ ] Failure   [ ] Water   [ ] Spiders   [ ] Crowds

    [ ] Hair loss   [ ] Injections   [ ] Sirens   [ ] Knives

    [ ] Other: _____

Your greatest fear: _____

Your most fearful moment: _____

_____

A crime or natural disaster you were a victim of: _____

_____

A crime or natural disaster you fear: _____

A sickness or disease you fear: _____

A reason for which you would seriously contemplate suicide: _____

_____

F E A R S

Your greatest fear about aging: _____

_____

When people first meet you, you are afraid they will think: _____

_____

A country you fear exploring: _____

Your greatest fear about marriage: _____

_____

Your greatest fear about having children: _____

_____

Something on your mind you are afraid to share: _____

_____

A plan or project you worry may fail: _____

_____

MEASURE YOUR FEARS

Pet a snake:

[ ] You did.   [ ] You would.   [ ] You would not.

Spend a week in an empty room:

[ ] You did.   [ ] You would.   [ ] You would not.

Ride in a hot-air balloon:

[ ] You did.   [ ] You would.   [ ] You would not.

Kill an animal *(fish, birds, and insects not included):*

[ ] You did.   [ ] You would.   [ ] You would not.

Sky dive:

[ ] You did.   [ ] You would.   [ ] You would not.

Sing in front of a huge audience:

[ ] You did.   [ ] You would.   [ ] You would not.

Scuba dive:

[ ] You did.   [ ] You would.   [ ] You would not.

Sit in the front seat of a roller coaster:

[ ] You did.   [ ] You would.   [ ] You would not.

M E A S U R E   Y O U R   F E A R S

Deliver a baby:

[   ] You did.   [   ] You would.   [   ] You would not.

Swim across the Amazon River:

[   ] You did.   [   ] You would.   [   ] You would not.

Change careers:

[   ] You did.   [   ] You would.   [   ] You would not.

Disappear for a long period of time:

[   ] You did.   [   ] You would.   [   ] You would not.

Walk through a forest alone at night:

[   ] You did.   [   ] You would.   [   ] You would not.

Join a space mission:

[   ] You did.   [   ] You would.   [   ] You would not.

Tell everyone what you honestly think of them:

[   ] You did.   [   ] You would.   [   ] You would not.

Call off your wedding:

[   ] You did.   [   ] You would.   [   ] You would not.

M E A S U R E   Y O U R   F E A R S

Walk naked through New York City for 10 minutes during rush hour:

[　] You did.　　　　[　] You would.　　　　[　] You would not.

Walk up to Mike Tyson and call him a girl:

[　] You did.　　　　[　] You would.　　　　[　] You would not.

Disarm a bomb:

[　] You did.　　　　[　] You would.　　　　[　] You would not.

Clean the outside windows of a skyscraper:

[　] You did.　　　　[　] You would.　　　　[　] You would not.

Draw a mustache on the *Mona Lisa* with a permanent marker:

[　] You did.　　　　[　] You would.　　　　[　] You would not.

Go on tour with Elvis Presley:

[　] You did.　　　　[　] You would.　　　　[　] You would not.

P S Y C H E

Your first name spelled backward is: _____

Write your first and last name initials on the lines below:

First initial: _____   Last initial: _____

Now quickly write five words that begin with each initial:

1 _____   1 _____

2 _____   2 _____

3 _____   3 _____

4 _____   4 _____

5 _____   5 _____

Something that has been on your mind lately:

_____

Something that has been on your mind for a long time: _____

_____

P S Y C H E

A period of time in your life when you felt protected: _____

_____

A period of time in your life when you felt overprotected: _____

_____

A period of time in your life when you felt unprotected: _____

_____

The first time you discovered power: _____

_____

The book that has affected you the most: _____

_____

The author who has affected you the most: _____

The piece of music that has affected you the most: _____

_____

The movie that has affected you the most: _____

_____

The event that has affected you the most: _____

_____

Three people who have affected you the most:

1 _____

2 _____

3 _____

Choose one existing book or movie title that defines you: _____

_____

Choose one existing book or movie title that defines your life: _____

_____

Even if you don't think you can draw well,
spontaneously create a self-portrait without being too serious.

You are most comfortable

[ ] alone. [ ] at work. [ ] socializing in groups.

[ ] spending time with one person. [ ] observing others.

When you really want to get to know someone, you say or ask: _____

_____

In social situations, you tend to

[ ] introduce yourself first. [ ] wait for others to introduce themselves.

When you are attracted to someone,

[ ] you like to be the cat. [ ] you like to be the mouse.

Your most romantic experience: _____

_____

The largest age difference you have had in a relationship: _____

Who was younger? _____

C A T   A N D   M O U S E

A person you successfully pursued in a short amount of time:

_____

A person you pursued over a long period of time:

_____

A person you unsuccessfully pursued over a long period of time:

_____

Something someone said or did that you found extremely attractive: _____

_____

Something someone said or did that you found frighteningly unattractive: _____

_____

A saying you have heard about men or women that you believe is true: _____

_____

_____

Two things that are appealing about women:

1 _____ *2* _____

Two things that are not appealing about women:

1 _____ *2* _____

Two things that are appealing about men:

1 _____ *2* _____

Two things that are not appealing about men:

1 _____ *2* _____

Your friends tend to be

[ ] male.   [ ] female.

[ ] older than you.   [ ] younger than you.

A physical trait you find attractive: _____

An intellectual ability that you find attractive: _____

_____

A personality trait that you find attractive: _____

You are irritated when people ask you: _____

_____

You love it when people ask you: _____

_____

Your secret passion: _____

Your longest grudge: _____

You truly believe it is possible to be with
one person for the rest of your life.   [ ] Yes   [ ] No

You like surprises.   [ ] Yes   [ ] No

Someone has thrown a surprise party for you.   [ ] Yes   [ ] No

You have thrown a surprise party for someone.   [ ] Yes   [ ] No

You regret that you never had a relationship with this person:

_____

A type of person you don't seem to get along with: _____

The star sign you are most compatible with: _____

The star sign you are least compatible with: _____

Your current spouse or partner's star sign: _____

Your previous spouse or partner's star sign: _____

You and your spouse or partner argue about this issue often: _____

_____

In your relationships   [   ] you seem to make most of the decisions.

                                     [   ] you do not seem to make most of the decisions.

At work   [   ] you seem to make most of the decisions.

                                       [   ] you do not seem to make most of the decisions.

C A T   A N D   M O U S E

The farthest distance you would travel now to be with someone you desire:

_____

The farthest distance you have ever traveled to be with someone you desired:

_____

What you enjoy most about having a committed relationship: _____

_____

What you dislike most about having a committed relationship: _____

_____

S E X U A L I T Y

Your sexiest feature: _____

The physical feature for which you are most often complimented:

_____

A place where you have always wanted to make love: _____

_____

A wonderful place where you have made love: _____

_____

A strange place where you have made love: _____

_____

A special place on your body that, when kissed or touched, feels unbelievably good:

_____

An unfulfilled sexual fantasy: _____

_____

S E X U A L I T Y

A fulfilled sexual fantasy: _____

_____

A fragrance that reminds you of someone with whom you have been intimate:

_____

The most perverted situation you have ever been in: _____

_____

The approximate number of sexual partners you have had:

[ ] under 10   [ ] 10-20   [ ] 20-30   [ ] 30-40

[ ] 40-50   [ ] over 50   [ ] over 100

You wish you had slept with

[ ] fewer people.   [ ] more people.

The largest age difference between you and a sexual partner: _____

Who was younger? _____

S E X U A L I T Y

The first time you achieved orgasm: _____

A person you regret sleeping with: _____

A person you regret not sleeping with: _____

You feel most attractive when: _____

A fantastic kisser you have known: _____

An uninhibited lover you have been with: _____

The worst lover you have experienced: _____

The book, song, or movie title that best describes your sexuality: _____

_____

Sex is: _____

_____

If you had more time alone, you would _____

_____

If you could change anything about the world, _____

_____

If you had a plane ticket to anywhere in the world, you would visit

_____

If you could live anywhere in the world, you would live in _____

_____

If you could visit any time period, you would choose _____

_____

If you could live in any time period, you would choose _____

_____

If you could ask God one question, it would be: _____

_____

If you could, you would spend time with this famous person:

_____

If you could be famous, you would like to be famous for _____

_____

If you could magically change one thing about your physical appearance, it would be

_____

If you were stranded on a desert island, you would want these three people with you:

1 _____

2 _____

3 _____

The first thing you would do on the desert island: _____

_____

The first thing you would do upon your return from the desert island:

_____

If you could change one law, _____

If you were in prison, you would spend your time _____

_____

If you could erase one memory, _____

_____

If you had extra money, _____

_____

If you had one million dollars, _____

_____

If you could choose your age of death, _____

If you could bring back one person from the dead, _____

_____

If you had wings, you would fly above _____

If you were the queen or king of your country, _____

_____

If you were a plant, you would be _____

If you were a beverage or cocktail, you would be _____

If you could start all over, _____

_____

Your current philosophy is: _____

_____

Something memorable that happened to you this month: _____

_____

Two things you did today:

1 _____

2 _____

Two people who occupy your thoughts the most:

1 _____

2 _____

Something you learned this week: _____

_____

Something you need to learn now: _____

_____

H E R E A N D N O W

Your most important goal right now: _____

It would be a relief right now if _____

_____

The best word to describe your current love life: _____

The best word to describe your current relationship: _____

The best word to describe your current work situation: _____

The best word to describe your life: _____

Your biggest obstacle right now: _____

You are happier today than in the past.   [ ] Yes   [ ] No

The most important thing in life: _____

_____

The last person you said "I love you" to: _____

A piece of wisdom you would pass on to a child: _____

_____

Now that you have answered all the questions in *All About Me*,
write one more question you would like to be asked:

_____

_____

The answer to your question is: _____

_____

_____